OUR GR★AT STATES

WHAT'S GREAT ABOUT

NORTH DAKOTA?

✳ Darice Bailer

↳ LERNER PUBLICATIONS COMPANY ✳ MINNEAPOLIS

CONTENTS

NORTH DAKOTA WELCOMES YOU! ✳ 4

Content Consultant: Mark S. Joy, PhD, Professor of American History, University of Jamestown, Jamestown, North Dakota.

Lerner Publications Company
A division of Lerner Publishing Group, Inc.
241 First Avenue North
Minneapolis, MN 55401 USA

For reading levels and more information, look up this title at www.lernerbooks.com.

Main body text set in ITC Franklin Gothic Std Book Condensed 12/15.
Typeface provided by Adobe Systems.

Library of Congress Cataloging-in-Publication Data

Bailer, Darice.
    What's great about North Dakota? / Darice Bailer.
        pages   cm. — (Our great states)
    Includes index.
    ISBN 978-1-4677-3389-2 (library binding : alkaline paper)
    ISBN 978-1-4677-4716-5 (eBook)
    1. North Dakota—Juvenile literature. I. Title.
F636.3.B27 2015
978.4—dc23   2014005181

Manufactured in the United States of America
2 - PC - 8/1/14

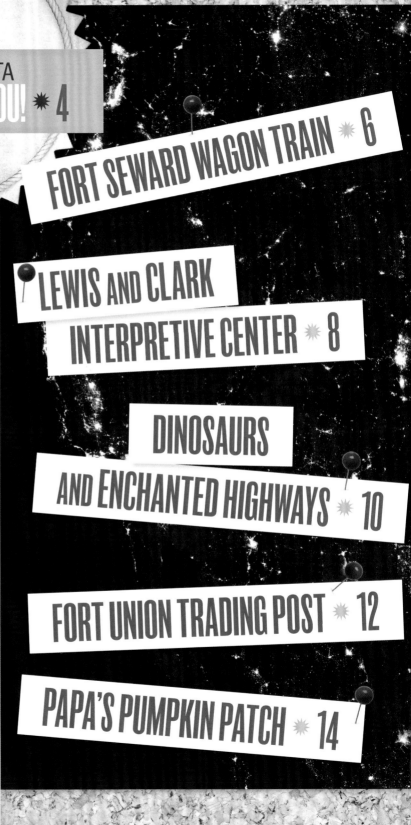

FORT SEWARD WAGON TRAIN ✳ 6

LEWIS AND CLARK INTERPRETIVE CENTER ✳ 8

DINOSAURS AND ENCHANTED HIGHWAYS ✳ 10

FORT UNION TRADING POST ✳ 12

PAPA'S PUMPKIN PATCH ✳ 14

JAMESTOWN * 16

THEODORE ROOSEVELT NATIONAL PARK * 18

FORT ABRAHAM LINCOLN STATE PARK * 20

BISMARCK * 22

KILLDEER MOUNTAIN ROUNDUP RODEO * 24

NORTH DAKOTA BY MAP * 27
NORTH DAKOTA FACTS * 28
GLOSSARY * 30
FURTHER INFORMATION * 31
INDEX * 32

NORTH DAKOTA Welcomes You!

A visit to North Dakota is a trip like no other. This is a place of cowboys and covered wagons. You'll see colorful American Indian powwows. Even dinosaurs once roamed this great state. North Dakota has fun for everyone. See where Lewis and Clark stopped along their journey. Take in the quiet beauty of Theodore Roosevelt National Park. Look out at the wide prairie and pale rocky bluffs. You'll understand why people are proud to call the Flickertail State home. So grab your cowboy hat and saddle up. Let's visit North Dakota!

CANADA

TURTLE
MOUNTAINS

N

Williston

Minot

Lake
Sakakawea

Little Missouri River

D R I F T

Devils Lake

P R A I R I E

James River

Sheyenne River

Grand Forks

R E D   R I V E R   V A L L E Y

Red River

MINNESOTA

MONTANA

B A D L A N D S

Dickinson

Missouri River

Mandan

Bismarck

Jamestown

West Fargo

Fargo

White Butte
(3,506 feet/1,069 m)

Miles
0   10   20   30   40

0   20   40   60
Kilometers

Red River

Wahpeton

SOUTH DAKOTA

Explore North Dakota's
parks and all the places
in between! Just turn the
page to find out about the
FLICKERTAIL STATE. >

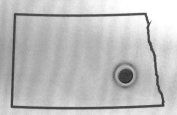

Live like a pioneer on the Fort Seward Wagon Train trip.

FORT SEWARD WAGON TRAIN

> What was it like to be a pioneer and ride in a covered wagon? Find out on the Fort Seward Wagon Train. Giddy up!

This modern wagon train re-creates the pioneer experience. It's a six-day trip that begins in June. The wagons start at Fort Seward Park near Jamestown. Experienced guides lead the trip. Dress up in pioneer clothes. Then climb aboard. You can even take a turn driving the horses.

Take a lunch break each day with the other guests. Fill up your plate near an old chuck wagon. You can help with chores, such as cooking dinner and building fires. At night, you'll sit around a campfire. Sing songs and swap stories with your fellow travelers. Then fall asleep under the stars. Wake up to a beautiful sunrise the next morning. Wagons roll!

Keep your eyes peeled for pheasants and other wildlife as you travel the North Dakota prairies.

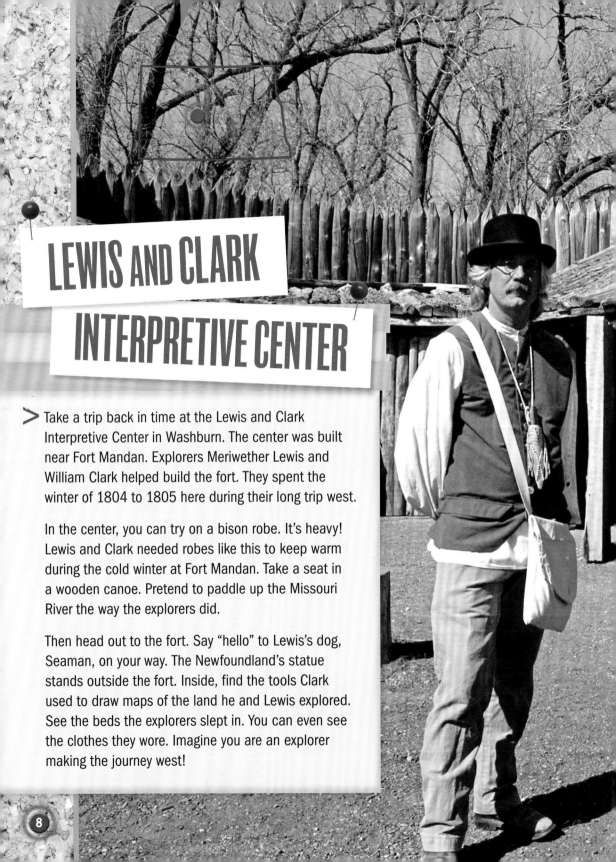

LEWIS AND CLARK INTERPRETIVE CENTER

> Take a trip back in time at the Lewis and Clark Interpretive Center in Washburn. The center was built near Fort Mandan. Explorers Meriwether Lewis and William Clark helped build the fort. They spent the winter of 1804 to 1805 here during their long trip west.

In the center, you can try on a bison robe. It's heavy! Lewis and Clark needed robes like this to keep warm during the cold winter at Fort Mandan. Take a seat in a wooden canoe. Pretend to paddle up the Missouri River the way the explorers did.

Then head out to the fort. Say "hello" to Lewis's dog, Seaman, on your way. The Newfoundland's statue stands outside the fort. Inside, find the tools Clark used to draw maps of the land he and Lewis explored. See the beds the explorers slept in. You can even see the clothes they wore. Imagine you are an explorer making the journey west!

William Clark was one of the famous explorers who helped build Fort Mandan in the 1800s.

LEWIS AND CLARK

In 1803, the United States bought the Louisiana Territory from France. This was land west of the Mississippi River. But the land had yet to be explored. President Thomas Jefferson asked his secretary, Meriwether Lewis, to lead an expedition there. Lewis set out with his friend William Clark. The expedition traveled through North Dakota as it explored the West from 1804 to 1806. The men reported on and mapped the frontier. This got people excited about settling the West.

DINOSAURS AND ENCHANTED HIGHWAYS

You'll see many interesting metal sculptures along the Enchanted Highway, including a giant grasshopper.

> Long before Lewis and Clark, dinosaurs roamed the Great Plains. Visit the Dakota Dinosaur Museum in Dickinson to see the remains of these giant reptiles. You can even see a triceratops skull that is 67 million years old! The museum is full of dinosaur bones. The museum also has an amazing collection of rocks and minerals from around the world.

Outdoors, drive along the Enchanted Highway. It's a 30-mile (48-kilometer) ride. Make sure to look out the window. You won't want to miss the giant metal sculptures. You can laugh at the giant grasshoppers and pheasants. Wave to the World's Largest Tin Family.

Some of the fossils on display at the Dakota Dinosaur Museum were found on land surrounding the museum.

FORT UNION
TRADING POST

> Fort Union Trading Post in Williston takes you back to North Dakota's old fur-trading days. The American Fur Company built this trading post in 1828. American Indians came here to trade furs to Europeans. The American Indians had many types of fur, from beaver to bison to grizzly bear. In exchange, American Indians got European goods. These may have included clothing, Italian beads, and cooking kettles.

Fort Union today is much like it was almost two hundred years ago. The staff members dress as fur traders and trappers. Listen to them talk about life at Fort Union. Be sure to ask about the Junior Trader program. Fill out the worksheet to earn a gold Fort Union Trading Post badge.

FORT BUFORD AND SITTING BULL

Fort Buford is an old military fort 2 miles (3.2 km) away from the trading post. Soldiers built Fort Buford in 1866. They hoped to protect the settlers and railroad workers from the Sioux American Indians. The railroad upset the Sioux. The construction chased away bison and wildlife. The Sioux relied on the bison for survival. Sioux chief Sitting Bull led several attacks on the fort. He surrendered to US officers at the fort in July 1881.

Animal furs were commonly traded between settlers and American Indians in the 1800s.

PAPA'S PUMPKIN PATCH

> You won't want to miss the fall fun at Papa's Pumpkin Patch. It is in Bismarck. And you've never seen a pumpkin patch like this one! It is full of fun activities.

Try to find your way out of the Bale Mazes. They have corners and alleyways made from more than eight hundred bales of straw. Slip down one of the slides on Slide Mountain. Then take a seat in the Great Pumpkin's Chair. You'll need to climb a ladder to reach it. The chair is nearly 15 feet (4.5 meters) tall!

Watch the Pumpkin Cannon fire pumpkins hundreds of feet into the air. Try to bury yourself in a Corn Crib. Corn kernels fill this sandbox almost 2 feet (0.6 m) deep. Then run across the logs in the Log Jam. See how you do on the obstacle course. Fly through the air on a zip line. Clip along on Grandpa Al's Horse-Drawn Hayride. Or climb on a pony for a ride.

How can you top all those activities? It's easy. Try Papa's famous pumpkin cookies! Don't forget to pick out a pumpkin before you leave.

NORTH DAKOTA CROPS

Agriculture is an important part of North Dakota's economy. Farms cover 90 percent of the state. North Dakota grows more barley, sunflower seeds, and wheat than any other state in the country. It also is known for beans, corn, honey, rye, and sugar beets. North Dakota exports many of these products to other states.

Take a train ride through the pumpkin patch.

JAMESTOWN

> No North Dakota vacation is complete without a stop in Jamestown. This old railroad town is full of history and fun. Have your camera handy on your way into town. You'll want to get your picture taken next to the biggest bison statue in the world. The bison's name is Dakota Thunder. You won't believe the size of this beast. It is 26 feet (8 m) tall and 46 feet (14 m) long.

Are you ready to see some real bison? Then head to Jamestown's National Buffalo Museum. It has a herd of about thirty bison. See if you can spot White Cloud. She is an extremely rare albino bison.

The National Buffalo Museum is located in Frontier Village. The village is full of fun activities. Take a ride on a stagecoach during the summer. Tour an old sheriff's office, a jail, or a fire department. See the train depot built in 1880. Then check out an 1878 grocery store. Peek inside the old schoolhouse. Can you imagine going to school here?

Pay a visit to White Cloud while you're in Jamestown.

NORTH DAKOTA RAILROADS

Railroads played an important role in North Dakota's history. Railroads brought settlers to the state. Trains carried supplies to people living on the frontier. North Dakota farmers used trains to ship their products to bigger cities in the East. Many towns grew up along the Northern Pacific Railway. Over time, it ran from Minnesota to the Pacific Ocean. The railway crossed North Dakota. Its workers lived in Jamestown in 1871 while laying tracks to Bismarck.

JAMESTOWN, ND

WORLD'S LARGEST BUFFALO 1959

THEODORE ROOSEVELT NATIONAL PARK

> If you like the outdoors, Theodore Roosevelt National Park is the place for you. It is located near the Missouri River. This area is known as the North Dakota Badlands.

Go for a hike on one of the park's many trails. Saddle up for a horseback ride on the Maah Daah Hey Trail. The name comes from a Mandan American Indian word meaning "grandfather." American Indians once hunted here.

Earn a Junior Ranger badge by learning more about the park. Pick up a free Junior Ranger Journal at any park visitor center. It's full of activities. Visit the park's website to print out a bingo card for your visit. Mark off the sights on the card as you see them.

Spend the night in nearby Medora. Watch the *Medora Musical*. This is the town's famous musical about Theodore Roosevelt. Kids can come onstage before the show begins. In the summer, you can even see live horses on the stage!

THEODORE ROOSEVELT

Theodore Roosevelt loved animals and the outdoors. He came to the North Dakota Badlands to hunt as a young man. His visit inspired him to protect the country's natural areas. Roosevelt became president of the United States in 1901. He formed the US Forest Service to protect wildlife and public land. He also created five new national parks. US president Harry Truman formed Theodore Roosevelt National Park in 1947.

Keep an eye out for elk and bison as you walk through the park.

FORT ABRAHAM LINCOLN STATE PARK

> History comes to life at Fort Abraham Lincoln State Park in Mandan. US soldiers built the fort on the Missouri River in 1872. They named it in honor of former US president Abraham Lincoln, who had been assassinated seven years earlier. The US government hoped to protect settlers and railroad workers on the frontier. About 650 men lived in the fort by 1874. It was one of the largest forts on the northern Great Plains.

US general George Armstrong Custer lived here. You can watch men dressed up like Custer's officers. Listen up! They might order you to march like a soldier. See Custer's house as it looked when he and his family lived here. Women dress in long prairie dresses. Tour guides talk as if they lived in Custer's time.

On-A-Slant Indian Village is part of the state park. Here you can see how the Mandan lived from about 1575 to 1780. See the tools they used for farming. Try to imagine what life was like for children growing up in the village!

General Custer became famous for his military service during the Civil War (1861–1865).

Step inside a replica of a Mandan earthen home.

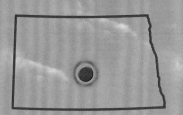

BISMARCK

Bismarck's capitol building is known as The Skyscraper on the Prairie.

> In late summer, Bismarck holds one of the biggest American Indian festivals in the nation. The United Tribes International Powwow takes place every Labor Day weekend. A powwow is a chance for people to get together, sing, dance, feast, and pray. You'll see more than fifteen hundred American Indians at this powwow. The powwow is loud and colorful. Listen to the chants. Hear the drums bang and the other instruments rattle.

There's plenty to do in Bismarck when the powwow is over. Climb aboard the *Lewis and Clark* riverboat. This paddleboat sails on the Missouri River. Then you can ride the elevator to the top of the North Dakota State Capitol. The capitol building is nineteen stories high.

Don't drive too far without visiting Salem Sue. This is the world's largest Holstein cow sculpture. She greets travelers coming into New Salem, 34 miles (54 km) west of Bismarck.

Many American Indians dress in traditional clothing with beads and feathers at the United Tribes International Powwow.

KILLDEER MOUNTAIN ROUNDUP RODEO

> While in North Dakota, be sure to go to a rodeo. Many cowboys once herded cattle in North Dakota. The state's grasslands are perfect for grazing cattle. Texas cattle companies liked to drive their herds here in the 1800s. The cowboys used ropes to keep the cows and calves in tow. The cowboys were proud of their riding and roping skills. They competed against one another at rodeos.

The Killdeer Mountain Roundup Rodeo is one of the oldest rodeos in North Dakota. It's held every summer. Watch a cowboy try to ride a bucking horse or bull here. Then check out the parade. Visit the petting zoo. Slip down the 18-foot (5.5 m) inflatable slide. Then chow down on some tasty barbecued ribs.

YOUR TOP TEN!

You've read about ten awesome things to do and see in North Dakota. What would your North Dakota top ten list include? What would you like to see and do if you visited the state? What attraction has you the most excited? These are all things to think about as you write your own list. Make your top ten list on a sheet of paper. Turn your list into a book. Illustrate it with drawings or pictures from the Internet or magazines.

A cowboy chases a calf at the Killdeer Mountain Roundup Rodeo.

Cowboys and cattle have been an important part of North Dakota's economy and culture since the 1800s.

25

> MAP KEY

⭐ Capital city

◯ City

◯ Point of interest

▲ Highest elevation

–··– International border

–·– State border

Visit www.lerneresource.com to learn more about the state flag of North Dakota.

NORTH DAKOTA

MONTANA

Williston

Missouri River

Fort Union Trading Post

Lake Sakakawea

Little Missouri River

Killdeer Mountain Roundup Rodeo (Killdeer)

Theodore Roosevelt National Park (Badlands)

Dickinson

Dakota Dinosaur Museum

BADLANDS

▲ White Butte (3,506 feet/1,069 m)

Enchanted Highway (runs for 30 miles/48 km, near Regent)

NORTH DAKOTA BY MAP

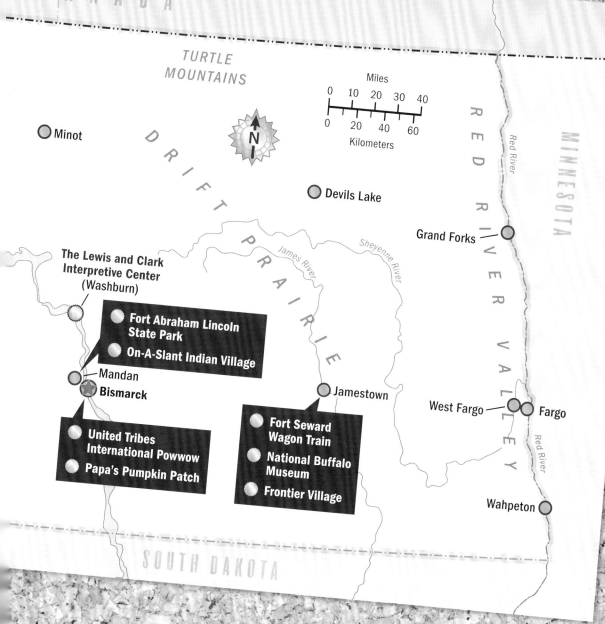

CANADA

TURTLE MOUNTAINS

Miles
0   10   20   30   40

0   20   40   60
Kilometers

N

Minot

DRIFT PRAIRIE

Devils Lake

RED RIVER VALLEY

Red River

MINNESOTA

James River

Sheyenne River

Grand Forks

The Lewis and Clark
Interpretive Center
(Washburn)

**Fort Abraham Lincoln
State Park**

On-A-Slant Indian Village

Mandan

Bismarck

**United Tribes
International Powwow**

Papa's Pumpkin Patch

Jamestown

**Fort Seward
Wagon Train**

**National Buffalo
Museum**

Frontier Village

West Fargo — Fargo

Red River

Wahpeton

SOUTH DAKOTA

NORTH DAKOTA FACTS

NICKNAME: Flickertail State

SONG: "North Dakota Hymn" by James W. Foley and Dr. C. S. Putnam

MOTTOS: Liberty and union, now and forever, one and inseparable

> **FLOWER:** wild prairie rose

TREE: American elm

BIRD: western meadowlark

ANIMAL: ground squirrel

> **FOOD:** milk

DATE AND RANK OF STATEHOOD: November 2, 1889; the 30th state

CAPITAL: Bismarck

AREA: 70,698 square miles (183,107 sq. km)

AVERAGE JANUARY TEMPERATURE: 7°F (−14°C)

AVERAGE JULY TEMPERATURE: 70°F (21°C)

POPULATION AND RANK: 701,345; 48th (2012)

MAJOR CITIES AND POPULATIONS: Fargo (109,779), Bismarck (64,751), Grand Forks (53,456), Minot (43,746), West Fargo (27,478)

NUMBER OF US CONGRESS MEMBERS: 1 representative, 2 senators

NUMBER OF ELECTORAL VOTES: 3

> **NATURAL RESOURCES:** clay, coal, gravel, lignite, natural gas, oil, petroleum, sand

> **AGRICULTURAL PRODUCTS:** barley, cattle, rye, sugar beets, sunflowers, wheat

MANUFACTURED GOODS: computer and electronics products, construction and farm machinery, food products, petroleum products

STATE HOLIDAYS AND CELEBRATIONS: North Dakota State Fair

GLOSSARY

agriculture: farming

albino: an animal born with milky-white skin and white or colorless fur

assassinate: to kill someone who is important or well known

bison: a large North American animal, sometimes called a buffalo, with a big, shaggy head; short horns; and a humped back

chuck wagon: a wagon carrying a stove and food for cooking

economy: the system in which goods are bought and sold in a place

expedition: a journey or trip with a special purpose

export: to send a product to another place to sell there

frontier: a region on the edge of the settled part of a country

powwow: an American Indian ceremony or social gathering

prairie: a large area of flat or rolling grassland

rodeo: a show of cowboy skills, such as riding and roping

LERNER

SOURCE™

Expand learning beyond the printed book. Download free, complementary educational resources for this book from our website, www.lerneresource.com.

FURTHER INFORMATION

Go West across America with Lewis and Clark Game
http://www.nationalgeographic.com/west
What was it like to go west with Lewis and Clark? You'll soon find out! You're offered choices along the route. For example, Sioux warriors seize one of your boats and draw their arrows. What should you do?

Gondosch, Linda. *Where Did Sacagawea Join the Corps of Discovery? And Other Questions about the Lewis and Clark Expedition*. Minneapolis: Lerner Publications, 2011. This book answers questions about the Lewis and Clark expedition and what it discovered.

Manning, Phillip Lars. *Dinomummy: The Life, Death, and Discovery of Dakota, a Dinosaur from Hell Creek*. Boston: Kingfisher Publications, 2007. In 2000, scientists uncovered a very special dinosaur in Hell Creek Formation in North Dakota. It was Dakota, a mummified duck-billed dinosaur! This is Dakota's story.

North Dakota
http://www.kidskonnect.com/subjectindex/33-places/states/198-north
-dakota.html
Do you want to know more about North Dakota? This site has fast facts about North Dakota and links to more information about the state, including its history and activities you can do there.

Theodore Roosevelt National Park
http://www.nps.gov/thro/index.htm
Visit the National Park Service's official website for Theodore Roosevelt National Park to learn more about the park's history and its many fun activities.

Watson, Galadriel Findlay. *North Dakota: The Peace Garden State*. New York: AV2 by Weigl, 2012. This book has more information about what makes North Dakota great.

INDEX

agriculture, 15

Bismarck, 14, 17, 22
bison, 8, 12, 16

cattle, 24
Clark, William, 4, 8–10, 22
cowboys, 4, 24
Custer, George Armstrong, 20

Dakota Dinosaur Museum, 10
dinosaurs, 4, 10

Enchanted Highway, 10

Fort Abraham Lincoln State Park, 20
Fort Buford, 12
Fort Mandan, 8
Fort Seward Wagon Train, 6
Fort Union Trading Post, 12

Jamestown, 6, 16–17
Jefferson, Thomas, 9

Killdeer Mountain Roundup Rodeo, 24

Lewis, Meriwether, 4, 8–10, 22
Lewis and Clark Interpretive Center, 8
Lincoln, Abraham, 20

Mandan American Indians, 18, 20
maps, 5, 26–27
Medora, 18

National Buffalo Museum, 16
North Dakota Badlands, 18–19

On-A-Slant Indian Village, 20

Papa's Pumpkin Patch, 14
powwows, 4, 22

railroads, 17
Roosevelt, Theodore, 4, 18–19

Sioux American Indians, 12
Sitting Bull, 12

Theodore Roosevelt National Park, 4, 18–19
Truman, Harry, 19
United Tribes International Powwow, 22

PHOTO ACKNOWLEDGMENTS

The images in this book are used with the permission of: © Jerry Hopman /Thinkstock, pp. 1, 19 (bottom), 21 (bottom); © sakakawea7/Thinkstock, pp. 4, 5 (bottom), 22; © Laura Westlund /Independent Picture Service, pp. 5 (top), 26–27; © Michael Burton/Thinkstock, p. 6; © Dave G. Houser/Corbis, pp. 6–7; © Wolfgang Kruck/Shutterstock Images, p. 7; © Connie Ricca/Corbis/Glow Images, pp. 8–9, 12–13, 20–21; © Mighty Sequoia Studio/Shutterstock Images, p. 9 (top); Library of Congress pp. 9 (bottom) (LC-USZ62-17372), 12 (HABS ND,53 -FOBUF,1--4), 17 (LC-USF34-057896-D), 19 (top) (LC-DIG-ppmsca-35950), 21 (top) (LC-DIG-cwpb-05340), 25 (right) (LC-USZ62-56804); USDA, p. 10; © Andre Jenny/Stock Connection Worldwide /Newscom, pp. 10–11; © Will Kincaid/AP Images, p. 11; © Zack Frank/Shutterstock Images, p. 13; © Rolf Fischer/Thinkstock, pp. 14–15; © venturecx/iStockphoto, p. 15 (top); © Mike McCleary/The Bismarck Tribune/AP Images, p. 15 (bottom); © Joseph Sohm/Glow Images, p. 16; © Daniel M. Silva/Shutterstock Images, pp. 16–17; © Rruntsch/Shutterstock Images, pp. 18–19; © AdStock RF/ Shutterstock Images, pp. 22–23; © Franz Marc Frei/LOOK-foto/Glow Images, p. 23; © Tom Bean/Corbis/Glow Images, pp. 24–25; © Tom Bean/Corbis, p. 25 (left); © Filip Bjorkman/Shutterstock Images, p. 26; © Ken Schulze/iStockphoto, p. 29 (top); © Danilin/iStockphoto, p. 29 (middle top); © AT/Thinkstock, p. 29 (middle bottom); © Gary Milner/ iStockphoto, p. 29 (bottom).

Cover: National Park Service (Ft. Union); © kjscrafts/Bigstock.com (buffalo); © Richard Cummins/Lonely Planet Images /Getty Images (dinosaur); North Dakota Tourism/Gene Kellogg (rodeo); © Laura Westlund/Independent Picture Service (map); © iStockphoto.com/fpm (seal); © iStockphoto.com/vicm (pushpins); © iStockphoto.com/benz190 (corkboard).